Mammals of Northwestern South Dakota

by Kenneth W. Andersen

The mammalian fauna of the western Dakotas and adjacent Montana is relatively poorly known. Few published reports have dealt with mammals from this part of the Northern Great Plains, and none of these involved detailed study of a restricted area. The present report summarizes information gathered in Harding County, northwestern South Dakota, and includes material on the more than 50 species of mammals that are known to occur there.

Harding County has an area of approximately 2700 square miles (Fig. 1). The county first was organized in 1881, but the present boundaries were not fixed until 1908. Physiographically, it lies in that part of the Missouri Plateau frequently termed the "Cretaceous Table Lands." The general topography is one of rolling hills and flats--mostly range land vegetated by short grasses and sage--broken by spectacular buttes and hills that rise 400 to 600 or more feet above the surrounding plains. These monadnocks are "... part of a system of Tertiary erosional remnants standing above the Late Cretaceous rocks of northwestern South Dakota...," according to Lillegraven (1970:832), who went on to point out: "The butte tops are flat and grass-covered. The western sides are being actively cut away by slumping, and the topography below the western cliff walls is hummocky with sparse vegetation. The eastern flanks of the tables are, by contrast, less cliff-forming and less slumped and are generally well forested with coniferous and deciduous trees." Slim Buttes, the North and South Cave Hills, the East and West Short Pine Hills, and the Long Pine Hills, which barely enter the county north of Camp Crook, comprise the pine-clad buttes; other prominences, such as Table Mountain and Sheep Buttes, are all but nude of coniferous cover. The highest point in the county, "Harding Peak," is 4019 feet above sea level.

Sediments underlying northwestern South Dakota include rocks assignable to the Pierre (shale), Fox Hills (sand), and Hell Creek formations of Cretaceous age and the Ludlow and Tongue River formations of the Paleocene. These rocks may be exposed at the surface, but usually are overlain by relatively thin soils that are mostly derived from them; the best soil in the county for agricultural purposes is the loessal sandy or silty loam in the northeastern quarter, which is derived from Tongue River sediments (Baker, 1952).

The climate of northwestern South Dakota is characteristic of the northern part of the interior grasslands of North America--that is, the winters are cold and the summers hot and dry. Weather data for the period 1896-1967 at Camp Crook are representative of those gathered at the several stations maintained in the county. At Camp Crook the mean temperature for January is 17.3 F, whereas that for July is 71.2 F; precipitation averages 13.17 inches annually, most falling in the months of April through September; snowfall amounts to an average of 33.2 inches per year and is recorded from every month from September through May (Climatogeography of the United States, no. 20-39, Camp Crook, South Dakota, 1969).

Major surface drainage systems in Harding County include the Little Missouri River, which flows northward through most of the western part of the county, the South Fork of the Grand River, which originates in the east-central part of the county and flows generally eastward, and by the North Fork of the Moreau River, which originates in the south and drains in a southeasterly direction. Permanent standing surface water was virtually unknown prior to the development of artificial impoundments.

Vegetation of the grassland areas in the county is typical of that found throughout the semi-arid Northern Great Plains. Cover on upland soils, especially those that are clayey in substance, generally is sparse; areas along water courses and well-watered sites elsewhere tend to have denser stands of grasses such as bluestem (Andropogon). Dominant grasses of upland are gramma, buffalo grass, wheat grass, stipa, and tickle grass. Sage (Artemisia) and numerous forbs are prominent in many areas. These grasslands are used extensively for grazing of sheep and cattle.

The wooded buttes mentioned above are at least in part within the boundaries of Custer National Forest and support western yellow pine (Pinus ponderosa) and junipers (Juniperus sp.). In some ravines and other protected sites there are groves of deciduous trees such as cottonwood, aspen, boxelder, ash, hackberry, elm, dogwood, and hawthorn, usually associated with shrubs such as buckbrush, chokeberry, plum, currant, and gooseberry. These groves frequently are associated with small springs, as the one in Deer Draw of the Slim Buttes. The major water courses and their tributaries are essentially treeless, although occasional stands of cottonwoods and other deciduous trees and shrubs occur in some places--for example along the Little Missouri near Camp Crook. Some representative habitats in Harding County are illustrated in Figs. 2-8.

Our interest in Harding County dates from August of 1960, when one of us (Jones) and Robert R. Patterson visited the area briefly and obtained a small collection of mammals. Subsequently, field parties from the Museum of Natural History collected mammals in the county in the periods 14-30 June 1961, 23 March-11 April 1963, 5-7 July 1965, and 13 May-11 June 1968. Incidental collection also occurred in the extreme western part of the county in the period 29 June-24 July 1970 when a group was working primarily in the Long Pine Hills of adjacent Carter County, Montana.

There are few published references to mammals in Harding County. Visher (1914), in an early biological survey of the area, listed 40 species of mammals, but his accounts are mainly of historic value. Subsequently, publications by Bailey (1915), Young (1944), Goldman (1944), Over and Churchill (1945), Jones and Genoways (1967), and Henderson et al. (1969) have recorded mammals from the county.

ACCOUNTS OF SPECIES

Fifty-three species of mammals known from Harding County, South Dakota, are treated in the accounts that follow. Appended is a brief discussion of 10 additional species that may be found there. In most accounts, specimens that have been examined (a total of 644) are listed in telegraphic style preceding remarks; localities are arranged from north to south in such lists. Unless otherwise noted, specimens are housed in the Museum of Natural History. All measurements are in millimeters (those of embryos are crown-rump lengths) and weights are given in grams.

Order Chiroptera

~Myotis evotis evotis~ (H. Allen, 1864)

Long-eared Myotis

Specimens examined (20).--NW 1/4 sec. 15, R. 5 E, T. 22 N, 2; 5 mi. N, 2 mi. W Camp Crook, 1; 10 mi. S, 5 mi. W Reva, 16; 7 mi. S, 4-1/2 mi. E Harding, 1.

The long-eared myotis is not uncommon in and around wooded buttes. The species may be mostly limited to these areas; an individual of unknown sex found dead in a small stream southeast of Harding (several miles south of the East Short Pine Hills) is the only specimen not taken in such a situation. North of Camp Crook, on the eastern edge of the Long Pine Hills, several M. evotis used an abandoned shed as a night roost in the summer of 1970; one was captured in a bat trap set at one of the entrances to the shed.

Females obtained on May 29 and June 17 and 19 carried single embryos that measured 3, 14, and 15, respectively. A male young of the year taken on August 6 was nearly of adult size. Testes of two May-taken males measured 4 and 2, whereas those of one taken on July 17 and another captured on August 3 measured 6.0 and 7.5, respectively.

Of seven adults collected in the period August 3 to 6, three females and two of four males were in fresh pelage; molt was nearly completed on the two remaining males. A male taken in mid-July was in an early stage of molt. New pelage is pale yellowish brown in contrast to the golden brown pelage of specimens taken in May and June.

Chiggers, Leptotrombidium myotis (Ewing), were found on the ears of one long-eared myotis.

~Myotis leibii ciliolabrum~ (Merriam, 1886)

Small-footed Myotis

Eight males of this saxicolous species were shot or netted as they foraged over a small man-made pond in wooded Deer Draw in the Slim Buttes, 10 mi. S and 5 mi. W Reva--six in late June and two in early August. Probably this bat will be found in rocky areas elsewhere in the county. One specimen taken on June 23 was molting over much of the body.

~Myotis lucifugus carissima~ Thomas, 1904

Little Brown Myotis

Specimens examined (27).--2 mi. N, 5 mi. W Ludlow, 1; NW 1/4 sec. 15, R. 5 E, T. 22 N, 4; NE 1/4 sec. 24, R. 8 E, T. 21 N, 20; 4 mi. S, 7 mi. W Ladner, 1; 10 mi. S, 5 mi. W Reva, 1.

This bat is widely distributed in northwestern South Dakota and was the only species of Myotis reported by Visher (1914:91) in his early natural history survey of Harding County. We took specimens from several of the wooded buttes and also in areas well-removed from timber; one was shot, for example, as it foraged over the Little Missouri River in the extreme western part of the county. On May 28, 1968, a barn was located in which an incipient maternal colony (several hundred adult females) roosted between double rafters supporting a metal roof. The owner of the barn, Robert Parks of Ralph, stated that bats have utilized this place as a summer roost for several years. The barn stands adjacent to the nearly treeless Big Nasty Creek, which flows through the hilly terrain of the northeastern section of the county.

Fourteen of 20 females taken from the colony each carried a single embryo (crown-rump lengths measured 2 to 11 with a mean of 5.4). The other six were not visibly pregnant upon gross examination but had enlarged uteri, possibly indicating recent implantation. Of the remaining females from Harding County, three collected on May 29 had enlarged uteri, whereas two collected in late June evidenced no gross reproductive activity. A male obtained May 29 had testes that measured 4.

Ectoparasites obtained from this species include chiggers, Leptotrombidium myotis (Ewing), a tick, Ornithodoros kelleyi Cooley and Kohls, fleas, Myodopsylla gentilis Jordan and Rothschild and M. insignis (Rothschild), and an unidentified species of mite.

~Myotis volans interior~ Miller, 1914

Long-legged Myotis

Specimens examined (43).--2 mi. N, 5 mi. W Ludlow, 4; NW 1/4 sec. 15, R. 5 E, T. 22 N, 12; 10 mi. S, 5 mi. W Reva, 27.

The long-legged myotis is one of the commonest bats of the wooded buttes, accounting for almost half of all chiropterans taken in these areas. Most of our specimens were shot as they foraged among trees and over water in the evening; a few were captured in mist nets.

Uteri of eight females obtained in the period May 23 to 31 were enlarged; two females collected on June 29 carried single embryos that measured 20 and 22. A lactating female was taken on August 3, but three other adult females taken early in the same month evidenced no reproductive activity. Testes measured 2 to 4 in three May-taken males and 4 in each of two from June.

Two males obtained June 16 and 23 were molting as evidenced by new hairs under the old pelage over much of the body.

Myotis volans that we examined for ectoparasites harbored chiggers, Leptotrombidium myotis (Ewing), and fleas, Myodopsylla gentilis Jordan and Rothschild.

~Lasionycteris noctivagans~ (LeConte, 1831)

Silver-haired Bat

A single female, which contained two embryos that measured 4, represents the only record of a silver-haired bat from Harding County. This specimen was shot at dusk on June 1, 1968, as it foraged over a small pond in Deer Draw of the Slim Buttes (10 mi. S and 5 mi. W Reva). Several other bats believed to be of this species were seen at the same place that evening. We initially assumed that these were late migrants, but recent findings indicate that this species is a common summer inhabitant of the Long Pine Hills in adjacent Carter County, Montana, and likely, therefore, also a resident in favored sites in Harding County.

~Eptesicus fuscus pallidus~ Young, 1908

Big Brown Bat

Specimens examined (11).--NW 1/4 sec. 15, R. 5 E, T. 22 N, 3; 7 mi. N, 2 mi. W Camp Crook, 3300 ft., 2; 10 mi. S, 5 mi. W Reva, 6.

The big brown bat is a common inhabitant of the Slim Buttes and North Cave Hills, where individuals were shot or netted as they foraged over water or among trees late in the evening.

Two May-taken females had enlarged uteri and one taken on July 8 was lactating. The testes of a May-taken male measured 5, whereas those of one obtained in early July measured 9. One of two males shot on August 4 was a young of the year; the other, an adult, was in fresh pelage as was an adult male shot on July 8. The July-taken lactating female and three June-taken specimens were in old pelage. Several specimens were parasitized on the ears by chiggers, Leptotrombidium myotis (Ewing).

~Lasiurus cinereus cinereus~ (Palisot de Beauvois, 1796)

Hoary Bat

The hoary bat seemingly is an uncommon summer resident of Harding County as but one specimen, a non-pregnant female, has been taken there. This bat was shot on the evening of June 22, 1961, in the Slim Buttes as it foraged over a small pond in Deer Draw (10 mi. S and 5 mi. W Reva).

~Plecotus townsendii pallescens~ (Miller, 1897)

Townsend's Big-eared Bat

Specimens examined (4).--2 mi. S, 3-1/4 mi. W Ludlow (Ludlow Cave), 2 (1 SDSU); 10 mi. S, 5 mi. W Reva, 2.

This big-eared bat evidently is uncommon in northwestern South Dakota. Of the four specimens examined, two were taken at Ludlow Cave and two were taken in June in the southern part of Slim Buttes--a female shot as it foraged over a pond in Deer Draw and another female netted over a water tank at Summit Spring about a half mile south of Deer Draw.

Ludlow Cave, in the caprock on the southeastern edge of the North Cave Hills, was formed by water erosion, resulting in numerous pockets and crevises in the ceiling and walls. The cave faces northwest; the mouth measures approximately 10 feet in diameter. A few feet from the entrance the cave narrows and approximately 50 feet back it is no more than three feet in diameter, although in the first 30 feet or so the ceiling varies from 10 to 15 feet in height. A thorough search of this cave on June 18, 1961, revealed one bat, a male Plecotus, which was shot from the ceiling about 15 feet from the entrance. No bats were found when the cave was visited on May 16 and again on June 4, 1968. Visher (1914:92) reported that several Plecotus were found there in early September, 1912. Probably Ludlow Cave, along with the several abandoned coal mines in the county, serves as a hibernaculum for some species of bats.

Order Lagomorpha

~Lepus townsendii campanius~ Hollister, 1915

White-tailed Jack Rabbit

Specimens examined (15).--NW 1/4 sec. 23, R. 1 E, T. 23 N, 1; sec. 24, R. 1 E, T. 22 N, 1; 2 mi. N, 2 mi. E Ladner, 1; 4 mi. S, 7 mi. W Ladner, 2; 10 mi. S Ladner, 1; 6 mi. N, 2-1/2 mi. W Camp Crook, 1; 2 mi. N Buffalo, 1; sec. 30, R. 3 E, T. 19 N, 1; SW 1/4 sec. 26, R. 2 E, T. 19 N, 1; 10 mi. S, 5 mi. W Reva, 3; 12 mi. S, 5 mi. W Reva, 1; 17 mi. S, 4 mi. W Reva, 1.

This jack rabbit is abundant throughout the areas of short grass in the county and individuals occasionally utilize grassy slopes of buttes. Extensive favorable habitat and the paucity of natural predators resulting from control operations probably are the principal factors favoring the heavy concentrations of this hare noted by all of our field parties.

A female examined on May 21 carried five fetuses and each of two others examined late in May carried six; all fetuses were nearly of the same size (110 to 120) and were completely covered with hair. A female obtained on May 31 appeared to have recently weaned young and females examined on June 5 and 17 were lactating. A female shot on June 28 and another taken on July 12 proved to be approximately half grown, although young of the year collected on June 16, 26, and 28 were nearly of adult size.

In late March of 1963, white-tailed jack rabbits were molting to summer pelage from the white pelage of winter.

~Sylvilagus audubonii baileyi~ (Merriam, 1897)

Desert Cottontail

Specimens examined (12).--2 mi. N, 5 mi. W Ludlow, 2; 10 mi. S, 4 mi. W Ladner, 1; 7 mi. N, 2-1/2 mi. W Camp Crook, 3300 ft., 1; 5 mi. W Buffalo, 1; 10 mi. S, 5 mi. W Reva, 7.

The desert cottontail is a common inhabitant of the uplands of Harding County, especially where varied local relief and in some instances brushy vegetation provide suitable cover. A female shot on May 26 in a dense stand of pines in the North Cave Hills carried five embryos that measured 75, another taken on July 4 was pregnant with six embryos that measured 18, and two females collected on June 16 and another on June 24 carried seven embryos that measured 32, 40, and 45, respectively. Two subadults collected in late June and two collected in early August were nearly full grown. The testes of an adult male obtained on March 28 measured 50.

The male mentioned above was completely in winter pelage. Adults taken on June 16, 23, and 24 had almost completed molt to summer pelage, but each retained some evidence of active hair replacement, most often over the shoulders; a pregnant female obtained on July 4 had only partially completed the molt to summer pelage. An adult female in summer pelage that was taken on August 4 was inexplicably molting on the sides and over the shoulders.

A May-taken female was parasitized by fleas, Cediopsylla inaequalis (Baker).

~Sylvilagus floridanus similis~ Nelson, 1907

Eastern Cottontail

Specimens examined (2).--4 mi. S, 7 mi. W Ladner, 1; 10 mi. S, 5 mi. W Reva, 1.

This rabbit is uncommon in northwestern South Dakota and evidently is strictly associated with riparian habitats. Our only specimens were taken along the Little Missouri River, where thickets and small cottonwood trees were prevalent, and at the edge of a thicket in spring-fed Deer Draw of the Slim Buttes.

A female obtained on June 26 carried eight embryos that measured 26, and was in process of seasonal molt. Testes of a male shot on May 20 measured 35.

Order Rodentia

~Eutamias minimus pallidus~ (J. A. Allen, 1874)

Least Chipmunk

Specimens examined (31).--2 mi. N, 5 mi. W Ludlow, 15; NW 1/4 sec. 15, R. 5 E, T. 22 N, 2; 2 mi. S, 3-1/4 mi. W Ludlow, 2; NW 1/4 sec. 32, R. 1 E, T. 20 N, 1; 9 mi. S, 7 mi. W Reva, 1; 10 mi. S, 5 mi. W Reva, 9; NE 1/4 sec. 8, R. 8 E, T. 16 N, 1.

The least chipmunk is common in the buttes and associated badlands where it most frequently inhabits rocky areas. Visher (1914:88) reported E. minimus from Harding County ("abundant in badlands"), but his paper has been overlooked by most subsequent workers. Visher's mention of a chipmunk from the mouth of the Moreau River in north-central South Dakota, incidentally, would seem to be in error, as would the report by Over and Churchill (1945:28) of Eutamias inhabiting "... thickets along the Little Missouri River of Harding County."

Females evidently bear but one litter annually (in late May) in northwestern South Dakota and young are weaned by the latter part of June. Females taken on May 15 and 19 carried embryos (five measuring 30 and three measuring 28, respectively). A lactating female with five placental scars was obtained on May 24, but eight adult females taken after June 23 previously had weaned young. Juveniles were collected on June 24 and 25. Testes of two adult males collected in mid-May measured 11 and 18, but males taken in summer had much smaller testes.

In late spring, most adult least chipmunks molt from the worn, drab-gray pelage of winter to a brighter, more tawny summer pelage, but molt in a few females, perhaps originally delayed by reproductive activity, continues well into the summer months. Of seven specimens taken between May 15 and 24, two (one male and one lactating female) were in an early stage of molt, whereas the remainder were in winter pelage. Nine specimens (four females and five males) taken in mid- and late June were molting, but two females collected then were in winter pelage, and three animals, two males and a female, had completed molt to summer pelage. One adult female taken on August 5 had yet to complete molt to summer pelage. In our material, the first indication of molt from winter to summer pelage appears on the top of the head and the cheeks. Thereafter, molt proceeds posteriorly over the shoulder region and more or less evenly along the back and sides. In two specimens, small patches of molt preceded the general molt line. Molt on the venter apparently begins after molt on the dorsum approaches completion, but we could discern no definite pattern; on four specimens, hair was being replaced on the venter in scattered patches.

An August-taken young of the year engaged in post-juvenal molt had new adult pelage in a vague hour-glass pattern in the dorsal trunk region as well as on the cheeks and anterior part of the head. It was actively molting on top of the head, between the ears, over the shoulders, laterally behind the front feet, and along the sides, and had old pelage on the rump. Ventrally, the new adult pelage was evident only along the midline.

One adult male examined for ectoparasites harbored a tick, Dermacentor andersoni Stiles, and fleas, Monopsyllus eumolpi Rothschild.

~Spermophilus tridecemlineatus pallidus~ J. A. Allen, 1874

Thirteen-lined Ground Squirrel

Specimens examined (22).--2 mi. N, 5 mi. W Ludlow, 5; 19 mi. N, 1 mi. E Camp Crook, 2; 2 mi. S, 2 mi. W Ladner, 1; 6-1/2 mi. N, 2 mi. W Camp Crook, 1; 1/2 mi. W Reva, 3; 4 mi. S, 1/2 mi. W Reva, 1; 6 mi. W Reva, 7; 15 mi. S, 4 mi. W Reva, 1; 7 mi. S, 4-1/2 mi. E Harding, 1.

Ground squirrels are common in areas of short grass; we observed them most frequently along roadways and fencerows in otherwise overgrazed flats. Many of our specimens were shot or taken in break-back traps baited with rolled oats in just such situations.

Young from the first litters of the year were above ground by late June and represented the largest segment of the population at that time; for example, only three of 17 individuals collected from June 20 to 27 were adults. Adult females collected on June 20 and July 7 had enlarged mammae but were no longer lactating.

Time of emergence from hibernation in northwestern South Dakota is unknown, but many ground squirrels were active in the last week of March, 1963. A male obtained on March 28 had testes that measured 27 and was in full winter pelage, which is easily distinguished from the shorter, darker pelage of summer.

~Cynomys ludovicianus ludovicianus~ (Ord, 1815)

Black-tailed Prairie Dog

Specimens examined (5).--Sec. 25, R. 3 E, T. 22 N, 2; 1-1/2 mi. W Buffalo, 1; 1/2 mi. W Camp Crook, 3200 ft., 2.

The extensive flatlands of short grasses on relatively deep soils provide ideal habitat for the black-tailed prairie dog in Harding County. Visher (1914:89) mentioned extensive colonies along "flats" of streams and reported one "town" west of the Little Missouri River that covered several sections and another "on the table of the West Short Pine Hills." Recently, emphasis on control of numbers of prairie dogs in the area has reduced many formerly extensive colonies to small, disjunct units. According to Robert Kriege (personal communication, 1968), a "town" of approximately 3000 acres, about five miles east of the Little Missouri River (in R. 2 E, T. 21 N), is the largest remaining in the county. Thirteen other colonies then known to him ranged in approximate size from 25 to 300 acres.

White-colored prairie dogs apparently are not uncommon in some areas of the county and local residents reported to us a number of instances of sighting such individuals. One "town" located 7-1/2 mi. N and 12 mi. W Ladner, in the northwestern corner of the county, contained at least six families of white individuals, congregated together at the edge of the colony, in the spring of 1968. White prairie dogs also were noted by one of our field parties in 1963 in a "town" formerly located 7-1/2 mi. W Buffalo.

~Tamiasciurus hudsonicus dakotensis~ (J. A. Allen, 1894)

Red Squirrel

Visher (1914:88) reported that he obtained a red squirrel in the Long Pine Hills, along the western border of Harding County, in July of 1910 and noted that the species had been reported to him as occurring also in the West Short Pine Hills. Visher's record evidently has been overlooked by subsequent cataloguers (see, for example, Hall and Kelson, 1959: map 257). Insofar as we can ascertain, T. hudsonicus does not now occur on any of the pine-clad buttes and ridges of the county, although the species is present in relatively dense stands of ponderosa pine in the Long Pine Hills of adjacent Carter County, Montana, at a place only a few miles west of the South Dakota border. Probably some individuals stray into the relatively small and sparsely-wooded areas of the Long Pine Hills that extend eastward to the north of Camp Crook.

On the basis of color, specimens we have examined from the Long Pines clearly are assignable to T. h. dakotensis rather than to T. h. baileyi, substantiating in part the statement of the distribution of dakotensis published by Miller and Kellogg (1955:263).

~Thomomys talpoides bullatus~ Bailey, 1914

Northern Pocket Gopher

Specimens examined (22).--NE 1/4 sec. 22, R. 1 E, T. 23 N, 1; 7 mi. N, 2-1/2 mi. W Camp Crook, 3300 ft., 3; Camp Crook, 1; 10 mi. S, 5 mi. W Reva, 10; 10 mi. S, 4 mi. W Reva, 4; 2 mi. S, 5 mi. E Harding, 2; Crow Buttes, 1 (USNM).

The northern pocket gopher probably occurs in most areas of northwestern South Dakota where the soil is sufficiently deep for constructing burrows, but we found it commonest in the lower grassy slopes of buttes and in relatively sandy areas along some of the major streams.

A female obtained on June 20 contained two embryos that measured 3. Testes of an adult male trapped on May 18 measured 19 and those of one taken on July 6 measured 9. Juveniles were collected in both May and June.

Bailey (1915:102) referred a specimen from Crow Buttes to T. t. bullatus, but Swenk (1941:3), in the original description of T. t. pierreicolus, suggested that this same specimen "probably" was referable to the latter because he assumed it came from soils of the Pierre series. However, Baker (1952:8) included the Crow Buttes in the Hell Creek formation and, in any event, one of us (Jones) examined the specimen in question and found it clearly referable to the subspecies bullatus. Over and Churchill (1945:32) erroneously assigned pocket gophers from northwestern South Dakota to two different subspecies (bullatus and clusius), referring at least one individual from Harding County to T. t. clusius.

Fleas, Dactylopsylla ignota (Baker), were found on one individual examined. Molting adults were taken in each month from May through August.

~Perognathus fasciatus fasciatus~ Wied-Neuwied, 1839

Olive-backed Pocket Mouse

Specimens examined (16).--2 mi. N, 5 mi. W Ludlow, 3; 4 mi. S, 7 mi. W Ladner, 9; 10 mi. S, 5 mi. W Reva, 1; 14 mi. S, 4 mi. W Reva, 2; 15 mi. S, 4 mi. W Reva, 1.

This pocket mouse is not uncommon in areas of short grass and sage in Harding County. None of five adult females taken late in June was pregnant or lactating, but three had enlarged mammae indicative of reproductive activity earlier in the spring, to which young of various sizes in our series also attest. Active molt was evident on adults taken on June 19, 26, and 28.

Our specimens are intergrades between Perognathus fasciatus fasciatus and the paler P. f. olivaceogriseus. Average external measurements of seven adults (two males and five females) are: total length, 138.0 (130-150); length of tail, 65.3 (59-74); length of hind foot, 17.1 (15-18.5); length of ear (six specimens only), 6.8 (6-7); weight in grams (five specimens only), 12.9 (11.2-14.6). Selected cranial measurements of the two males and two of the females are, respectively, as follows: occipitonasal length, 24.0, 23.2, 23.5, 22.3; interorbital breadth, 4.9, 5.2, 5.0, 5.0; mastoid breadth, 13.0, 13.1, 12.2, 11.9; length of maxillary toothrow, 3.3, 3.3, 3.1, 3.4.

~Perognathus hispidus paradoxus~ Merriam, 1889

Hispid Pocket Mouse

An adult female, not reproductively active, that was trapped in rather sparsely vegetated rangeland to the southwest of Slim Buttes (14 mi. S and 4 mi. W Reva) on July 19, 1961, is the only specimen of the hispid pocket mouse on record from Harding County. Other species of small mammals taken in the same or adjacent traplines were Perognathus fasciatus, Dipodomys ordii, Reithrodontomys megalotis, Peromyscus maniculatus, and Onychomys leucogaster.

A single individual reported from Wade, Grant Co., North Dakota, by Bailey (1927:123), approximately 100 miles to the northeast, is the only specimen known from a more northerly locality.

~Dipodomys ordii terrosus~ Hoffmester, 1942

Ord's Kangaroo Rat

Specimens examined (13).--NE 1/4 sec. 22, R. 1 E, T. 23 N, 6; 2 mi. N, 5 mi. W Ludlow, 1; 2 mi. S, 11 mi. W Reva, 1; 14 mi. S, 4 mi. W Reva, 4; 15 mi. S, 4 mi. W Reva, 1.

Ord's kangaroo rat is found in sparsely vegetated flatlands throughout Harding County, although it appears to be uncommon except in localized areas of relatively sandy soils. Five of seven specimens taken from June 18 through 24, 1961, were young of the year, as were three of six individuals trapped on May 31, 1968. One adult female (81.1 grams) obtained on May 31 was lactating and had four placental scars, whereas another that weighed 67.2 grams evidenced no recent reproductive activity. An adult male (67.9 grams) taken on May 31 had testes that measured 9; those of a subadult male (46.5 grams) taken on the same date measured only 6.

The two May-taken adult females mentioned above still were completely in winter pelage, but the adult male trapped at the same time was molting. An adult male (57.2 grams) obtained on June 22 had completed molt save for a small patch between the ears and immediately behind the head.

~Castor canadensis missouriensis~ Bailey, 1919

Beaver

Specimens examined (2).--Sec. 22, R. 1 E, T. 20 N, 1; 32 mi. SE Buffalo, 1.

According to local residents, the beaver is common along many of the water courses in the county. One of our two specimens came from a tributary of the Little Missouri River north of Camp Crook and the other was taken from a tributary of the Moreau River in the southeastern part of the county. Robert Kriege of Buffalo reported to us that beaver are not restricted to wooded areas, but frequently inhabit streams and more or less permanent impoundments bordered by grassland. In such places they are said to construct bank dens and eat principally sage and forbs.

Visher (1914:89) reported this species along the Little Missouri River, Boxelder Creek, the forks of Grand River, Bull Creek, and "Devil's Gulch" in the North Cave Hills, and figured (pl. 6) a dam on Rabbit Creek. We have observed evidence of beaver activity along the Little Missouri River southwest of Ladner and along aspen-wooded stream banks in the Short Pine Hills, where in the spring of 1963 abundant sign was found.

~Reithrodontomys megalotis dychei~ J. A. Allen, 1895

Western Harvest Mouse

Specimens examined (27).--NE 1/4 sec. 22, R. 1 E, T. 23 N, 1; 4 mi. S, 7 mi. W Ladner, 3; 2 mi. N, 5 mi. W Ludlow, 7; 1/2 mi. W Reva, 14; 10 mi. S, 5 mi. W Reva, 1; 14 mi. S, 4 mi. W Reva, 1.

The western harvest mouse was taken commonly in stands of tall grasses and forbs, particularly along roadways and fencerows. Occasional individuals were trapped in areas of mixed shrubs and grasses. Four pregnant females taken in late June carried the following number of embryos (crown-rump lengths in parentheses): seven (4), six (5), six (10), five (4). Three adult males taken in the same period had testes that measured 7, 7, and 8, whereas those of two May-taken males measured 12 and 6.

Molt from winter to summer pelage was in progress, from anterior to posterior, on both the dorsum and venter of many May- and June-taken animals. Some individuals had completed molt, or had but a small patch of winter pelage remaining on the rump, as early as the last week in June.

~Reithrodontomys montanus albescens~ Cary, 1903

Plains Harvest Mouse

Specimens examined (3).--2 mi. N, 5 mi. W Ludlow, 2; 1/2 mi. W Reva, 1.

This harvest mouse is uncommon in northwestern South Dakota, although the species probably occurs sparingly in upland grassy habitats throughout Harding County. Our specimens, along with one in the collections of the University of Michigan Museum of Zoology, not previously reported, from 11 mi. S Mandan, Morton Co., North Dakota, represent the northernmost known records of this mouse.

A young adult female, obtained on June 21, carried three embryos that measured 17 and was in summer pelage; an adult male taken on June 27 still was in a worn winter pelage.

At the locality 1/2 mi. W Reva, where traps were set in sparse to relatively lush grassy areas along South Dakota Highway 20, the following small mammals were taken in the same trapline (or adjacent lines) in which one plains harvest mouse was captured: Spermophilus tridecemlineatus pallidus, Reithrodontomys megalotis dychei, Peromyscus maniculatus nebrascensis,

Microtus ochrogaster haydenii, and Microtus pennsylvanicus insperatus.

~Peromyscus leucopus aridulus~ Osgood, 1909

White-footed Mouse

Seven adults of this woodland inhabitant were trapped along shrub-covered banks of the spring-fed stream and small impoundment in Deer Draw of the Slim Buttes (10 mi. S and 5 mi. W Reva). Deciduous trees grew in the bottom of the draw, but the slopes above supported ponderosa pine and juniper. No white-footed mice were found along the generally treeless tributaries of the Moreau and Grand rivers to the east of Slim Buttes nor were these mice found along the Little Missouri River or in likely-looking habitat in the North Cave Hills. The P. leucopus of Deer Draw likely represent, therefore, an isolated segment of a formerly much more broadly distributed population of white-footed mice on the Northern Great Plains in post-Wisconsin times. Other such populations may exist in Slim Buttes and perhaps elsewhere in the county. Zapus hudsonius and Microtus pennsylvanicus were trapped in Deer Draw in association with white-footed mice.

Females collected on June 15 and August 7 were lactating and one taken on June 20 contained six embryos that measured 15. Two males taken on June 2 had testes that measured 12 and 15. These two males and a lactating female taken on June 15 still were in winter pelage, whereas a non-breeding female obtained on June 15 and a male and female (pregnant) trapped on June 20 were in summer pelage or an advanced stage of molt to that pelage. A lactating female taken on August 7 was in summer pelage excepting that what definitely appeared to be new winter pelage was present on the head, cheeks, and below the ears, and molt was evident adjacent to these areas.

Selected average (and extreme) measurements of the seven adults from Deer Draw are: total length, 184.4 (175-199); length of tail, 77.4 (70-88); length of hind foot, 21.1 (20-22); length of ear, 16.7 (16-18); greatest length of skull, 27.8 (27.0-28.4); zygomatic breadth, 14.6 (14.0-14.9); least interorbital width,

4.1 (4.0-4.3); length of maxillary toothrow, 4.2 (4.0-4.4). Three males and two non-pregnant females weighed 34.9, 34.6, 30.5, 32.2, and 31.4 grams, respectively.

~Peromyscus maniculatus nebrascensis~ (Coues, 1877)

Deer Mouse

Specimens examined (214).--19 mi. N, 1 mi. E Camp Crook, 5; 18 mi. N Camp Crook, 2; 2 mi. N, 5 mi. W Ludlow, 58; 4 mi. S, 7 mi. W Ladner, 14; 9 mi. N, 3 mi. W Camp Crook, 3400 ft., 3; 7 mi. N, 2-1/2 mi. W Camp Crook, 3300 ft., 2; NW 1/4 sec. 32, R. 1 E, T. 20 N, 4; 1/2 mi. W Reva, 2; SW 1/4 sec. 30, R. 7 E, T. 18 N, 5; 9 mi. S, 7 mi. W Reva, 3; 10 mi. S, 5 mi. W Reva, 64; 14-15 mi. S, 4 mi. W Reva, 33; 2 mi. S, 5 mi. E Harding, 16; 7 mi. S, 4-1/2 mi. E Harding, 3.

The deer mouse is the most abundant and widespread small mammal in northwestern South Dakota. We took specimens in all terrestrial habitats, although the species was commonest in upland situations such as grassy fencerows, rocky areas, and hillsides supporting shrubs, juniper, or pine.

Adult mice in reproductive condition were taken in each month from May through August, although most of our information is for the months of May and June. In the last half of May, seven pregnant females carried an average of 5.0 (4-6) embryos that ranged in crown-rump length from 2 to 10; three others taken in the same period had six, six, and three recent placental scars, and another was lactating. Twenty-three males collected late in May had testes that measured 5 to 15 (average 10.2). In the last half of June, 19 females contained an average of 4.9 (2-7) embryos that ranged in size from 3 to 30 in crown-rump length, and two more were lactating; seven males obtained in the period June 15-25 had testes that averaged 8.7 (8-10).

Additionally, we took lactating females on July 6, July 7, and August 7, and two individuals with recent placental scars on August 5. Twenty adult males collected in the period July 6 to 18 had testes that averaged 9.3 (6-11.5), whereas those of two taken on August 4 and 5 measured 10 and 12, respectively. Young animals in juvenal pelage were captured in each month, May through August, the earliest being taken on May 20. The first female young of the year that was found carrying embryos was trapped on June 16.

Molt from winter to summer pelage is evident on some specimens taken as early as the latter part of May, but most individuals from that period and from the first part of June still retained winter pelage. By the last half of June, some mice had completed (or nearly so) the seasonal molt, but many retained at least some worn pelage of winter into the first week of July.

Two distinctive maturational pelages are seen in our material--juvenal and post-juvenal or subadult, which generally resembles adult pelage (of season) in texture but is duller of color. Collins (1918) for P. maniculatus, Hoffmeister (1951) for P. truei, and Brown (1963) for P. boylii, among others, have described maturational pelages and sequence of maturational molts similar to those observed in our specimens.

Deer mice from Harding County clearly are referable to P. m. nebrascensis (rather than to the smaller and paler P. m. luteus, which occurs to the east and southeast), even though adults average somewhat paler than adults of typical populations of that subspecies. A tick of the Ixodes ochotonae-angustus complex was obtained from one specimen.

~Onychomys leucogaster missouriensis~ (Audubon and Bachman, 1851)

Northern Grasshopper Mouse

Specimens examined (4).--NE 1/4 sec. 22, R. 1 E, T. 22 N, 2; 2 mi. N, 5 mi. W Ludlow, 1; 14 mi. S, 4 mi. W Reva, 1.

We found the grasshopper mouse uncommon in Harding County. All four of the mice listed as examined were trapped in areas supporting sage and short grasses, with relatively little ground cover.

Three of our four specimens are immature--two males collected on May 31 (testes 10, 12) and a female taken on June 25. An adult male trapped on June 18 was in winter pelage, but molt was underway on the crown, between the ears, and over the upper back and shoulders.

~Neotoma cinerea rupicola~ J. A. Allen, 1894

Bushy-tailed Wood Rat

Specimens examined (8).--2 mi. N, 5 mi. W Ludlow, 5; 12 mi. N Buffalo, 1 (USNM); 7 mi. N, 2-1/2 mi. W Camp Crook, 3300 ft., 1; 2 mi. S, 5 mi. E Harding, 1.

This woodrat is relatively uncommon, yet widely distributed, in northwestern South Dakota. The species probably occurs throughout the rocky areas in the hills and buttes of Harding County, and also frequents abandoned or little-used buildings and feed stations for livestock. All of our specimens were trapped in rocky habitats, but in many such places we trapped unsuccessfully for Neotoma cinerea, even though some sign of its presence frequently was evident. Five of our seven specimens (all taken late in June or early in July) are young of the year in grayish pelage. An adult male trapped on July 14 had testes that measured 14.

Over and Churchill (1945:40) mentioned a specimen, which they referred to the subspecies N. c. cinerea, that "probably came from the Slim Butte area of Harding County." Visher (1914:89) recorded the species as "plentiful and general" in the county.

~Microtus ochrogaster haydenii~ (Baird, 1858)

Prairie Vole

Specimens examined (40).--NE 1/4 sec. 22, R. 1 E, T. 23 N, 1; NW 1/4 sec. 15, R. 5 E, T. 22 N, 1; 2 mi. N, 5 mi. W Ludlow, 4; 4 mi. S, 7 mi. W Ladner, 19; 1/2 mi. W Reva, 2; SW 1/4 sec. 30, R. 7 E, T. 18 N, 3; 10 mi. S, 5 mi. W Reva, 10.

The prairie vole is the most abundant of the three microtines that are known from Harding County. Our specimens came primarily from areas of relatively dense grasses, such as those found in stream bottoms and along fencerows. At two places, along a fencerow 1/2 mi. W Reva and in Deer Draw, 10 mi. S and 5 mi. W Reva, Microtus ochrogaster and the meadow vole, M. pennsylvanicus, were trapped together.

Nine females taken late in May and in June carried an average of 4.4 (3-6) embryos that averaged 14.8 (4-25) in crown-rump length. Each of two lactating females taken in late May had six placental scars. Testes of seven adult males taken in May and June averaged 13.1 (12-16) in length.

~Microtus pennsylvanicus insperatus~ (J. A. Allen, 1894)

Meadow Vole

Specimens examined (14).--1/2 mi. W Reva, 1; 10 mi. S, 5 mi. W Reva, 12; 7 mi. S, 4-1/2 mi. E Harding, 1.

This vole evidently is limited in Harding County to habitats of dense grass and forbs adjacent to water. We failed to trap the species in some areas that appeared to be suitable for occupancy.

Two females, collected on May 15 and June 2, contained three and six embryos, respectively, that measured 15. One female with five placental scars (May 15) and two with six (May 16, June 2) also were trapped, and a lactating female was captured on June 20. Testes of two adult males taken in spring (May 18 and June 2) measured 15, and those of one weighing 45.6 grams that was taken early in June measured 17.

~Ondatra zibethicus cinnamominus~ (Hollister, 1910)

Muskrat

The muskrat is common in Harding County. Half a century ago Visher (1914:89) noted that it was "Fairly plentiful along the streams having deep permanent 'holes'."

Seven adults, all in winter pelage, were taken late in March from a pond near the west side of Slim Buttes (5 mi. S and 14 mi. E Buffalo). Testes of three adult males measured 17, 19, and 22; of three females, none evidenced reproductive activity.

~Mus musculus~ Linnaeus, 1758

House Mouse

The house mouse evidently is uncommon in rural environments in northwestern South Dakota. One subadult female was trapped along a "weedy" fencerow, 2 mi. N and 5 mi. W Ludlow.

~Zapus hudsonius campestris~ Preble, 1899

Meadow Jumping Mouse

Eleven specimens of this jumping mouse were taken from a relict population restricted to a shrub-grass habitat adjacent to a small spring-fed stream and impoundment in Deer Draw (10 mi. S and 5 mi. W Reva). Similar isolated populations may be present in the few other suitable mesic habitats in Harding County, but we have trapped extensively, yet unsuccessfully, for Zapus in such situations; specimens are known, however, from the Long Pine Hills and from along the Little Missouri River in adjacent Carter County, Montana. It is of interest that a relict population of Peromyscus leucopus also occurs in Deer

Draw.

The testes of two adult males obtained on June 3 measured 7, whereas those of one taken on May 16 measured 16. Seven embryos (measuring 8 in crown-rump length) were carried by a molting female trapped on June 16. Our specimens of Zapus, currently under study by Paul B. Robertson, appear to be intergrades between the subspecies campestris and intermedius, but resemble the former more closely than the latter.

~Erethizon dorsatum bruneri~ Swenk, 1916

Porcupine

Specimens examined (11).--NW 1/4 sec. 15, R. 5 E, T. 22 N, 1; 2 mi. N, 5 mi. W Ludlow, 3; 4 mi. S, 7 mi. W Ladner, 1; 10 mi. S, 4 mi. W Reva, 1; 10 mi. S, 5 mi. W Reva, 4; 2 mi. S, 5 mi. E Harding, 1.

The porcupine is a common resident of the pine-clad buttes of Harding County and individuals were occasionally encountered some distance from pines. We noted porcupines almost nightly in June of 1961 along the road that parallels the Slim Buttes to the east, and found a number that had been struck by automobiles along this and other roadways in, or adjacent to, wooded areas. Visher (1914:90) earlier reported Erethizon from Harding County.

Order Carnivora

~Canis latrans latrans~ Say, 1823

Coyote

Specimens examined (8).--North Cave Hills, 1; N of Slim Buttes, 1; N end Slim Buttes, 1; 6 mi. N, 4 mi. W Camp Crook, 2; W of East Short Pine Hills, 1; E of Short Pine Hills, 1; Sheep Mountain, 1.

The coyote population in Harding County and adjacent areas is low owing to an active predator control program that is supported by local ranchers and by state and federal agencies. Our field parties neither saw nor heard coyotes, although tracks were found at one or two places in March of 1963. According to Robert Kriege (personal communication), the few coyotes that do reside in the area find refuge in the most rugged parts of the hills and buttes. Visher (1914:90) reported that this carnivore was "generally considered as abundant." Our specimens all are skulls of individuals killed by a federal trapper in the winter of 1961-62.

~Canis lupus nubilus~ Say, 1823

Gray Wolf

Visher (1914:90) stated that wolves were "quite plentiful" in the early 1900's; he quoted figures for a two-month period in 1910 when a government trapper took five adults and 25 pups in the vicinity of the Short Pine Hills and two adults and 11 pups in the general area of the Cave Hills. According to local residents, wolves were common in Harding County in the 1920's. One (the famous "Three Toes") trapped 20 mi. NW Buffalo in July of 1925 had eluded capture for more than 13 years, and in that period caused an estimated $50,000 in damage to livestock (Young, 1944:259, 277). It seems likely that the skull of this animal, in the U.S. National Museum, is the one referred to by Goldman (1944:445).

Wolves apparently had become rare by about 1930. The last one known to have been killed in northwestern South Dakota was taken on January 27, 1945, near Red Elm, Ziebach County (Carl Cornell, personal communication). We have seen a photograph of this wolf, which was mounted and now is on display in Deadwood, South Dakota.

As noted by Goldman (1944:442), the subspecies nubilus probably is extinct.

~Vulpes vulpes regalis~ Merriam, 1900

Red Fox

Specimens examined (6).--1 mi. S, 5 mi. E Ladner, 3; 3 mi. S, 12 mi. E Ludlow, 1; 2 mi. W Camp Crook, 3200 ft., 1; 4 mi. S, 1 mi. E Buffalo, 1.

This fox was present, although apparently not abundant, in Harding County in the early part of this century (Visher, 1914:90). He reported knowledge of "two or three" that had been trapped in the county and further noted a report that red foxes were "not rare along the Lone Pines." Visher's paper evidently was overlooked by Hall and Kelson (1959: map 447), who did not include the western half of South Dakota within the distribution of the species. The only foxes observed by our field parties were two seen in July of 1970--one an immature animal held captive in Camp Crook and remains of another that had been killed on a county road about 18 miles north of that place. Five specimens that had been killed by hunters were acquired in March 1963 and an isolated skull was picked up west of Camp Crook in 1970.

There is a continuing demand from sheep ranchers in the county that foxes be controlled, yet this species seems to maintain considerably higher populations than does the coyote. According to federal trapper Robert Kriege (personal communication), dens of the red fox have been found principally in the badlands and in certain grassland areas, but rarely in the buttes proper. Records kept by Mr. Kriege indicate that litters are born in mid-March in Harding County. He estimated that over the past few years he has examined whelps from an average of 50 dens a year, but that more than 170 dens were found in the spring of 1963.

~Ursus americanus americanus~ Pallas, 1780

Black Bear

Visher (1914:91) reported that a black bear "was seen near the Cave Hills in July, 1910." He further noted: "Bears have been recently killed in the Long

Pine and Ekalaka forests [of adjacent Montana], but their day of extermination is here near at hand." We know of no other reports of this carnivore from the area.

~Ursus arctos horribilis~ Ord, 1815

Grizzly Bear

According to Visher (1914:91) a grizzly bear was killed in the early 1890's a short distance southwest of Camp Crook.

~Procyon lotor hirtus~ Nelson and Goldman, 1930

Raccoon

Specimens examined (10).--2 mi. N, 5 mi. W Ludlow, 4; 1/2 mi. W Reva, 1; 4 mi. E Reva, 2; NW 1/4 sec. 32, R. 1 E, T. 20 N, 3.

The raccoon evidently is one of the commonest carnivores in Harding County. On June 24, 1961, a den with three young (average total length, 429) was found in one of the numerous pockets eroded from the caprock of the North Cave Hills, and on May 21, 1968, another den, this one containing five young (average total length of three, 271), was found in a similar situation on the east edge of the Long Pine Hills. A female trapped on June 20, 1961, was lactating.

Three individuals that had been killed at Ralph, along nearly treeless Big Nasty Creek, were examined on May 28, 1968.

~Mustela frenata longicauda~ Bonaparte, 1838

Long-tailed Weasel

This mustelid seems uncommon in northwestern South Dakota. The only recent reports from Harding County that have come to our attention are of a female and four or five young that were found in a haystack "several years prior to 1963" (Robert Kriege, personal communication), and of several individuals seen by a rancher in a hay field along the Little Missouri about 7 mi. N Camp Crook during mowing operations in July 1970. Visher (1914:91) regarded the species as "quite common," and noted that "4 or 5 dead ones" were seen along roads in the summer of 1910.

~Mustela nigripes~ (Audubon and Bachman, 1851)

Black-footed Ferret

In a recent summary of the natural history of this species in South Dakota, Henderson et al. (1969) listed seven localities in Harding County (all in prairie dog "towns") at which ferrets had been sighted or trapped as follows (dates in parentheses): near Ladner (March, 1963); 17 mi. N Camp Crook (about 1956 or 1957); T. 20 N, R. 3 E (1964); T. 20 N, R. 4 E (winter, 1964); T. 19 N, R. 1 E (late November, 1966); T. 17 N, R. 8 E (summer, 1965); T. 15 N, R. 1 E (winter, 1963). These authors also reported a specimen in the U.S. National Museum (no. 243990) that was taken at Govert on November 1, 1923. Additionally, Wesley Broer, then the local game warden, reported to one of our parties that a ferret was seen on February 27, 1963, at a place 7 mi. N and 16 mi. W Buffalo.

Visher (1914) made no mention of this species in his report of the natural history of Harding County.

~Mustela vison letifera~ Hollister, 1913

Mink

Tracks of a mink were observed by a member of one of our field parties (T. H. Swearingen) in late March of 1963 at a pond 5 mi. S and 14 mi. E Buffalo, and one was reported to have been trapped in the same area the previous winter. Reports by local residents indicate that mink occur along the Little

Missouri River as well as streams on the north side of the North Cave Hills. Visher (1914:91) reported the species to be uncommon but he knew of one trapped in February of 1911 on Bull Creek.

~Taxidea taxus taxus~ (Schreber, 1778)

Badger

Specimens examined (4).--Sec. 25, R. 3 E, T. 22 N, 1; NE 1/4 sec. 28, R. 4 E, T. 19 N, 1; 4 mi. E Reva, 1; 10 mi. S, 2 mi. W Buffalo, 1.

Local residents regarded the badger as relatively common in the grasslands of Harding County, although this species was only rarely observed by members of our field parties. Visher (1914:91) reported it to be "quite common."

~Spilogale putorius interrupta~ (Rafinesque, 1820)

Spotted Skunk

We took no spotted skunks in northwestern South Dakota and both local residents and government trappers reported this species to be rare in the area. Visher (1914:91) indicated that it was "much more common than the large skunk" in the early part of this century.

~Mephitis mephitis hudsonica~ Richardson, 1829

Striped Skunk

Visher (1914:91) found this species to be "uncommon" in Harding County, as we did more than a half century later. Some local residents, however, reported this skunk to be fairly abundant. We took one specimen, an adult female having enlarged mammae that was captured on July 6, 1965, at a place 7 mi. S and 4-1/2 mi. E Harding, just south of the Short Pine Hills. Site records of several other striped skunks were obtained as follows: 14 mi. N Buffalo; 6 mi.

N and 2-1/2 mi. W Camp Crook; 5-1/2 mi. WNW Buffalo; 1-1/2 mi. S and 1/2 mi. E Buffalo; 4 mi. S Buffalo; 10 mi. SW Ralph; and 1 mi. S Reva.

~Lutra canadensis interior~ Swenk, 1920

Otter

We have no record of this species in Harding County other than Visher's (1914:91) report that an individual was "recently trapped along the Little Missouri River."

~Felis concolor hippolestes~ Merriam, 1897

Mountain Lion

This large cat likely occurred throughout northwestern South Dakota prior to settlement by white man. No specimens are available from Harding County, but Visher (1914:91) reported that an individual "visited the East Short Pines in the winter of 1910-11." It is doubtful that Felis concolor occurs in the area today, except possibly as an occasional transient.

~Lynx rufus pallescens~ Merriam, 1899

Bobcat

Specimens examined (3).--12 mi. N, 9 mi. W Buffalo, 1; 11 mi. N, 7 mi. W Buffalo, 1; 9 mi. N, 9 mi. W Buffalo, 1.

The bobcat, although not abundant, is generally distributed throughout Harding County, particularly in the buttes and badlands. Visher (1914:90) reported the species as common in the early part of this century. Our three specimens were shot in March 1963 by professional hunters sponsored by the Western South Dakota Sheepman Association, two from the air and one on the ground. Two other bobcats were killed in the same three-day period (March

25-27).

We tentatively assign our specimens to the subspecies pallescens owing to their pale color and the general agreement of their external and cranial measurements with those reported for other specimens of that race. Geographic variation in Lynx rufus from throughout the Northern Great Plains is poorly documented, however, and is in need of critical analysis. External measurements of the three specimens, all males (adult and two young adults, respectively), are: total length, 870, 925, 820; length of tail, 142, 176, 155; length of hind foot, 191, 192, 178; length of ear, 82, 84, 71; weight (pounds), 23, 17, 16. Respective lengths of testes were 30, 36, and 15. Selected cranial measurements of the adult and largest young adult are: condylobasal length, 113.7, 111.5; zygomatic breadth, 88.3, 83.7; interorbital constriction, 24.5, 23.5; length of nasals, 30.1, 30.8; length of maxillary toothrow, 37.7, 38.6.

Order Artiodactyla

~Cervus elaphus canadensis~ Erxleben, 1777

Wapiti or Elk

Visher (1914:87) reported that the last native elk in Harding County was killed in the Long Pine Hills in 1879, and also mentioned skulls picked up in the Cave Hills. The origin of a wapiti allegedly shot in the Slim Buttes in 1956 (Robert Kriege, personal communication) is unknown, but presumably this individual was a wanderer, possibly from the Black Hills to the south where elk were reintroduced some years ago.

~Odocoileus hemionus hemionus~ (Rafinesque, 1817)

Mule Deer

Specimens examined (6).--2 mi. N, 5 mi. W Ludlow, 1; 9 mi. N, 10 mi. W Buffalo, 2; 10 mi. S, 5 mi. W Reva, 3.

The mule deer is common in the buttes and adjacent badland areas of the county, and many were seen by members of each of our field parties. Local residents reported "black-tails" to be widespread in the area and State Game Protector Merritt Paukarbek reported to Andersen that even though hunting success was high in the autumn of 1967, there was no apparent reduction in numbers in the spring of 1968. In contrast, Visher (1914:88) found this species absent in Harding County in the early 1900's, and stated that it was "exterminated by 1900."

An adult female taken on June 26, 1961, in the North Cave Hills was molting and evidenced no indication of reproductive activity.

~Odocoileus virginianus dacotensis~ Goldman and Kellogg, 1940

White-tailed Deer

Specimen examined (1).--8-1/2 mi. N, 1-1/2 mi. E Camp Crook, 1.

The white-tailed deer is less abundant in northwestern South Dakota than is O. hemionus, but a number were seen by members of our parties (in Deer Draw of the Slim Buttes, for example), and local residents reported many sightings to us. Visher (1914:82) earlier recorded this species as once "fairly plentiful in the forest reserves" in Harding County, but stated that it had become rare when he made his biological survey of the area in 1910 and 1912.

~Antilocapra americana americana~ (Ord, 1815)

Pronghorn

Specimens examined (2).--Sec. 28, R. 8 E, T. 23 N, 1; 12 mi. S, 10 mi. W Buffalo, 1.

This species is the most conspicuous (and possibly the most abundant) ungulate in Harding County. It ranges throughout the county on flat and rolling grasslands where small groups, and occasionally herds of up to 50 individuals, were seen in 1960, 1961, 1963, 1968, and 1970. Visher (1914:88) reported that the pronghorn was common in the area until about 1900, but that it was near the point of extinction when he visited the county in 1910 and 1912.

~Bison bison bison~ (Linnaeus, 1758)

Bison

According to historical accounts (Anonymous, 1959), the bison was rare or absent in Harding County at the time of settlement in 1876. By the early 1880's, however, herds were of regular occurrence, and there is one record (op. cit.: 95-96) of thousands crossing the Little Missouri near Camp Crook in November of 1882.

One report has it that the last bison killed in the county was shot in the summer of 1884 (op. cit.: 73-74), but Visher (1914:88) reported that an "old settler" had seen "a small bunch in 1886." Visher also reported finding bison remains, probably in 1910 or 1912, to the northeast of the North Cave Hills and west of the South Cave Hills.

~Ovis canadensis auduboni~ Merriam, 1901

Mountain Sheep

According to Visher (1914:88), mountain sheep formerly inhabited all the areas of buttes in Harding County but were extirpated in the 1890's. Sheep Mountain, a large butte just below the south end of the Slim Buttes, was reported to be the last area in which these animals occurred. Over and Churchill (1945:54) mentioned both the Cave Hills and Slim Buttes as localities formerly inhabited by O. c. auduboni.

Early in 1961, the South Dakota Game Commission introduced 12 animals, four rams and eight ewes, from Alberta (subspecies O. c. canadensis) on the Slim Buttes, but none is known to have survived to 1968.

SPECIES OF UNVERIFIED OCCURRENCE

The ten species of mammals listed below are not known certainly to occur in Harding County, but there is a strong likelihood that some will be found in the area or once occurred there. Three were mentioned by Visher (1914) as having been seen or taken in the county at the time of, or prior to, his biological survey of 1910 and 1912, but his accounts were not supported by adequate documentation. In addition to the kinds listed, several other mammals, such as Keen's bat (Myotis keenii septentrionalis), the red bat (Lasiurus borealis borealis), or the least weasel (Mustela nivalis campestris) are known to occur near enough to the area that the possibility of their presence cannot be discounted.

~Sorex cinereus haydeni~ Baird, 1858.--No shrews presently are known from Harding County. This species almost certainly will be found in relatively mesic habitats there, however, as our field parties have taken specimens in adjacent Bowman County, North Dakota, and only a few miles to the west of the county in the Long Pines Hills of Montana.

~Sorex merriami merriami~ Dobson, 1890.--This shrew inhabits somewhat more xeric areas than most other members of the genus and surely occurs in northwestern South Dakota. Specimens are on record from western North Dakota and northwestern Nebraska, and in the summer of 1970 a field party from The University of Kansas took one but a half mile west of the Harding County (state) line in Carter County, Montana.

~Spermophilus richardsonii richardsonii~ (Sabine, 1822).--Visher (1914:88) reported that he saw individuals of this species "in the extreme northwestern corner" of Harding County. However, the limits of the presently known range of the species are approximately 150 miles distant from that area.

~Sciurus niger rufiventer~ E. Geoffroy St.-Hilaire, 1803.--The fox squirrel presently is unrecorded from much of the West River part of South Dakota. Hoffmann et al. (1969:589), however, recently have reported specimens from along the Yellowstone River in eastern Montana and this squirrel now may occur also along the Little Missouri River. It was not surprising, therefore, when residents of Camp Crook reported to us that in recent years they have seen what were believed to be fox squirrels along the Little Missouri near that town. Specimens now are needed to verify these reports.

~Lagurus curtatus pallidus~ (Merriam, 1888).--The sagebrush vole undoubtedly occurs, albeit probably uncommonly, in areas of sage in northwestern Harding County, because specimens have been taken recently a few miles north and west of the county in North Dakota and Montana, respectively. We trapped unsuccessfully (900 trap nights) for this vole on sage flats to the north of Camp Crook and west of the Little Missouri River in the summer of 1970. "Sign," which appeared to be that of Lagurus, was found in this area, but only Peromyscus maniculatus and Spermophilus tridecemlineatus were trapped there.

~Rattus norvegicus~ (Berkenhout, 1769).--No records of this introduced murid are available from northwestern South Dakota, but it seems likely that the species has reached the area.

~Vulpes velox~ (Say, 1823).--Visher (1914:90) reported seeing a swift fox "along the Little Missouri Valley in North Dakota" and further noted that an early settler [Sol Catron] had "trapped a few" in Harding County. Whatever the former status of this fox in northwestern South Dakota may have been, the species evidently does not occur in the area today, or is rare, and the subspecific status of V. velox throughout much of the Northern Great Plains is in question. A specimen obtained in February of 1970 at a place 9 mi. N and 2 mi. E Scranton, Slope Co., North Dakota, is the only swift fox taken north of Nebraska in recent years (Pfeifer and Hibbard, 1970:835).

~Urocyon cinereoargenteus ocythous~ Bangs, 1899.--Jones and Henderson

(1963:288) reported a gray fox from Deer Ear Buttes, Butte Co., South Dakota, approximately 15 miles south of the Harding County line. This species appears to have dispersed westward in recent years, and its future occurrence in the county is likely.

~Gulo gulo luscus~ (Linnaeus, 1758).--The wolverine probably occurred sparingly in northwestern South Dakota until the time of early settlement, but we know of no verified records from Harding County or surrounding areas. A recent report of a specimen taken south of Timber Lake, Dewey Co., South Dakota (Jones, 1964:283), indicates that it may again be found in the area.

~Lynx canadensis canadensis~ Kerr, 1792.--We have no reports of this species in Harding County save that Visher (1914:90) noted that local residents claimed specimens had "been taken recently in the Cave Hills." Hoffmann and Pattie (1968:53) reported that the lynx occurs presently in eastern Montana and we suspect that individuals may occasionally range into Harding County.

ZOOGEOGRAPHIC COMMENTS

Of the 53 mammals listed in the foregoing accounts, all but one (Mus musculus) are native North American species. These fall into five rather well-defined faunal groupings as outlined by Hoffmann and Jones (1970:364-365). A majority (27) can be characterized as "widespread species." Most of these have broad distributions over much of North America; a few do not, but are widely enough distributed that it is impossible to assign them with certainty to a more circumscribed assemblage. Mammals from northwestern South Dakota that can be characterized as widespread are: Myotis leibii, Myotis lucifugus, Eptesicus fuscus, Lasionycteris noctivagans, Lasiurus cinereus, Castor canadensis, Peromyscus maniculatus, Ondatra zibethicus, Erethizon dorsatum, Canis latrans, Canis lupus, Vulpes vulpes, Ursus americanus, Ursus arctos, Procyon lotor, Mustela frenata, Mustela vison, Taxidea taxus, Mephitis mephitis, Lutra canadensis, Felis concolor, Lynx rufus, Cervus elaphus, Odocoileus hemionus, Odocoileus virginianus, Antilocapra americana, and

Bison bison. The above list is composed mainly of volant or relatively large and mobile mammals, several of which occur also in Eurasia or range well into the Neotropics.

A few widespread species deserve special comment. Two, the pronghorn and bison, are typical inhabitants of the interior grasslands of North America and might be considered steppe species save for the fact that each has an extensive distribution beyond that region. Four other species, Erethizon dorsatum, thought of primarily as a mammal of coniferous forests, and Ursus arctos, Taxidea taxus, and Odocoileus hemionus, all more or less western taxa, are not so broadly distributed as are other members of this grouping. Of the five bats, three are year-round residents, but Lasiurus cinereus and evidently Lasionycteris noctivagans are migrants.

The remaining 25 kinds of mammals are representative of four regional faunal groupings as follows: boreomontane species (10), steppe species (nine), species with Sonoran affinities (four), and species of the eastern deciduous forest (two).

Boreomontane species.--Of the 10 mammals in this faunal group, three (Eutamias minimus, Tamiasciurus hudsonicus, and Microtus pennsylvanicus) are distributed both in the boreal forests to the north of the plains and in montane areas to the west. Six species (Myotis evotis, Myotis volans, Plecotus townsendii, Thomomys talpoides, Neotoma cinerea, and Ovis canadensis) are primarily montane in distribution and evidently reached northwestern South Dakota from the west in late Wisconsin or post-glacial times; all but the pocket gopher occur there now only in the vicinity of coniferous timber or rocky buttes. The remaining species, Zapus hudsonius, is a glacial "relic." The nearest populations now are far to the north, and this jumping mouse occupies only restricted habitats in northwestern South Dakota and adjacent regions. In Harding County, Z. hudsonius presently is known only from Deer Draw in the Slim Buttes.

Steppe species.--Taxa intimately associated with the Great Plains are: Lepus townsendii, Cynomys ludovicianus, Spermophilus tridecemlineatus, Perognathus fasciatus, Perognathus hispidus, Reithrodontomys montanus, Microtus ochrogaster, Mustela nigripes, and Spilogale putorius (subspecies interrupta). A few of these are endemic to the plains, but most occur in grassland habitats beyond the borders of the region. All clearly are well adapted to, and therefore presumably evolved in response to, the environment of the interior grasslands; this zoogeographic unit, then, is characterized by truly steppe species that have relatively narrow habitat requirements and largely concordant patterns of distribution.

The case of the spotted skunk deserves brief commentary. This species was not taken or observed by members of our field parties and local residents made no claim to its presence except for a few vague recollections of spotted skunks having been seen "years ago." Visher (1914:91), however, reported that Spilogale was much commoner than Mephitis in the early part of the century. However that may have been, Spilogale putorius, as currently understood, would be judged to be a widespread species except that recent evidence strongly suggests that the plains race (interrupta) is not of the same species as spotted skunks to the west (subspecies gracilis). Furthermore, the ranges of the two are not in contact. Whatever its ultimate specific affinities may be, S. p. interrupta clearly is a plains mammal, and thus is here considered in that zoogeographic unit.

Sonoran species.--Sylvilagus audubonii, Dipodomys ordii, Reithrodontomys megalotis, and Onychomys leucogaster are invaders to the Northern Great Plains from the Sonoran region to the southwest. The latter two, however, are rather broadly distributed on the Great Plains and their assignment as Sonoran species is somewhat arbitrary. It is of interest that as many as nine mammals with southwestern affinities occur as far north as southwestern South Dakota and adjacent Wyoming.

Eastern species.--Only Sylvilagus floridanus and Peromyscus leucopus can be identified as species primarily associated with the eastern deciduous forest. The former is limited in northwestern South Dakota to brushy habitats in riparian communities, whereas P. leucopus is restricted to relatively good stands of deciduous timber and presently is known to occur only in Deer Draw of the Slim Buttes.

Throughout its known range in the western part of the Northern Great Plains, P. leucopus is represented by small and disjunct populations associated with riparian deciduous timber. The known population nearest to Harding County is on the Black Hills to the south; next nearest are several isolated or semi-isolated populations along the Yellowstone River in eastern Montana. Presumably, this white-footed mouse spread northwestward into the western part of the plains region along river systems, in company with deciduous trees, in some post-glacial period when the climate was warmer and wetter than now. Subsequent drying altered substantially the distribution and perhaps composition of riparian forests, and isolated populations of P. leucopus evidently survived only in restricted areas, such as Deer Draw, many of them probably marginal habitat for the species.

Unverified species.--If the 10 species listed as of "unverified occurrence," it seems highly likely that as many as eight will be found to occur, or occurred within historic time, in Harding County. Among these eight are one steppe species (Vulpes velox), three with boreomontane affinities (Sorex cinereus, Gulo gulo, and Lynx canadensis), two (Sciurus niger and Urocyon cinereoargenteus) that are associated with the eastern deciduous forests, and two (Sorex merriami and Lagurus curtatus) that are Great Basin elements.

It is noteworthy that the last-mentioned faunal unit is not known to be represented in northwestern South Dakota.

ACKNOWLEDGMENTS

For assistance in the field, we are especially grateful to the students who were enrolled in the Field Course in Vertebrate Zoology at The University of Kansas in the summers of 1961, 1965, and 1970, and to M. A. Levy, R. R. Patterson, and T. H. Swearingen. In 1965 and 1970, the summer field course was supported in part by grants (GE-7739 and GZ-1512, respectively) from the National Science Foundation; Andersen was supported in the field in 1968 by a grant from the Kansas City Council for Higher Education. Personnel of the U.S. Forest Service (Sioux Division, Custer National Forest), particularly District Ranger Timothy S. Burns, were most helpful to us in the field, as were Wardens Wesley Broer and Merritt Paukarbek of the South Dakota Department of Game, Fish and Parks. Robert Kriege, Federal predator control agent stationed in Buffalo, was most generous in sharing with us his knowledge of rodents and carnivores in the area, and many present or former residents, particularly Carl Cornell and Spike Jorgensen, also provided useful information and were helpful in other ways.

Ectoparasites reported here were identified by Cluff E. Hopla (fleas), Richard B. Loomis (chiggers), and Glen M. Kohls (ticks). Other than mammals housed in the Museum of Natural History, we examined only three, two in the U.S. National Museum (USNM) and one in the collection at South Dakota State University, Brookings (SDSU).

LITERATURE CITED

ANONYMOUS

1959. Building an empire: a historical booklet on Harding County, South Dakota. Buffalo Times-Herald, 108 pp.

BAILEY, V.

1915. Revision of the pocket gophers of the genus Thomomys. N. Amer. Fauna, 39:1-136.

1927. A biological survey of North Dakota. N. Amer. Fauna, 49: vi + 1-226 [this publication is dated 1926, but actually was published on January 8, 1927].

BAKER, C. L.

1952. Geology of Harding County. Rept. South Dakota State Geol. Surv., 68:1-36 (mimeographed).

BROWN, L. N.

1963. Maturational molts and seasonal molts in Peromyscus boylii. Amer. Midland Nat., 70:466-469.

COLLINS, H. H.

1918. Studies of normal moult and of artificially induced regeneration of pelage in Peromyscus. Jour. Exp. Zool., 27:73-99.

GOLDMAN, E. A.

1944. Classification of wolves. Pp. 387-507, in The wolves of North America (S. P. Young and E. A. Goldman), Amer. Wildlife Inst., Washington, D.C., xx + 636 pp.

HALL, E. R., and K. R. KELSON

1959. The mammals of North America. Ronald Press, New York, 2: xxx + 1-546 + 79 and 2: viii + 547-1083 + 79.

HENDERSON, F. R., P. F. SPRINGER, and R. ADRIAN

1969. The black-footed ferret in South Dakota. South Dakota Dept. Game, Fish and Parks, Pierre, 37 pp.

HOFFMANN, R. S., and J. K. JONES, JR.

1970. Influence of late-glacial and post-glacial events on the distribution of Recent mammals on the Northern Great Plains. Pp. 355-394, in Pleistocene and Recent environments of the Central Great Plains (W. Dort, Jr., and J. K. Jones, Jr., eds.), Univ. Press of Kansas, Lawrence, xii + 433 pp.

HOFFMANN, R. S., and D. L. PATTIE

1968. A guide to Montana mammals.... Univ. Montana, Missoula, x + 133 pp.

HOFFMANN, R. S., P. L. WRIGHT, and F. E. NEWBY

1969. Distribution of some mammals in Montana. I. Mammals other than bats. Jour. Mamm., 50:579-604.

HOFFMEISTER, D. F.

1951. A taxonomic and evolutionary study of the pinon mouse, Peromyscus truei. Illinois Biol. Monogr., 21: ix + 1-104.

JONES, J. K., JR.

1964. Distribution and taxonomy of mammals of Nebraska. Univ. Kansas Publ., Mus. Nat. Hist., 16:1-356.

JONES, J. K., JR., and H. H. GENOWAYS

1967. Annotated checklist of bats from South Dakota. Trans. Kansas Acad. Sci., 70:184-196.

JONES, J. K., JR., and F. R. HENDERSON

1963. Noteworthy records of foxes from South Dakota. Jour. Mamm., 44:283.

LILLEGRAVEN, J. A.

1970. Stratigraphy, structure, and vertebrate fossils of the Oligocene Brule

Formation, Slim Buttes, northwestern South Dakota. Bull. Geol. Soc. Amer., 81:831-850.

MILLER, G. S., JR., and R. KELLOGG

1955. List of North American Recent mammals. Bull. U.S. Nat. Mus., 205: xii + 1-954.

OVER, W. H., and E. P. CHURCHILL

1945. Mammals of South Dakota. Univ. South Dakota Mus., 56 pp. (mimeographed).

PFEIFER, W. K., and E. A. HIBBARD

1970. A recent record of the swift fox (Vulpes velox) in North Dakota. Jour. Mamm., 51:835.

SWENK, M. H.

1941. A study of subspecific variation in the Richardson pocket gopher (Thomomys talpoides) in Nebraska, with description of two new subspecies. Missouri Valley Fauna, 4:1-8.

VISHER, S. S.

1914. Report on the biology of Harding County, northwestern South Dakota. Bull. South Dakota Geol. Surv., 6:1-103.

YOUNG, S. P.

1944. Their history, life habits, economic status, and control. Pp. 1-385, in The wolves of North America (S. P. Young and E. A. Goldman), Amer. Wildlife Inst., Washington, D.C., xx + 636 pp.